easy
barbecues

THE AUSTRALIAN
Women's Weekly

CONTENTS

Australian cup and spoon measurements are metric. A conversion chart appears on page 77.

Barbecuing is an easy method for everyday cooking, and has become incredibly popular in most households. Covered barbecues can be thought of as an outdoor oven for cooking just about any type of seafood, poultry or meat and most vegetables – even barbecuing joints of meat is easy these days. It's a fast and healthy way to cook, as there is little added fat. Marinate the meat before you go to work in the morning, and it's ready for the barbecue as soon as you get home.

Pamela Clark

Food Director

SPICY VEGETABLE KEBABS

prep & cook time 30 minutes makes 8
nutritional count per kebab 0.8g total fat
(0g saturated fat); 263kJ (63 cal);
8.3g carbohydrate; 3.8g protein; 3.7g fibre

1 trimmed corn cob (250g)
2 baby eggplants (120g), cut into
   3cm slices
1 large green capsicum (350g), cut into
   4cm pieces
1 large red capsicum (350g), cut into
   4cm pieces
8 large truss cherry tomatoes (250g)
200g button mushrooms
spicy tomato marinade
½ cup (125ml) tomato puree
2 tablespoons lime juice
1 tablespoon dark soy sauce
2 cloves garlic, crushed
1 long green chilli, chopped finely

1 Cut corn crossways into eight pieces. Steam
or microwave corn and eggplant, separately,
until tender; drain.
2 Make spicy tomato marinade.
3 Thread vegetables onto eight bamboo
skewers; coat with spicy tomato marinade.
4 Cook kebabs on heated oiled barbecue (or
grill plate), turning occasionally and brushing
with remaining marinade, until vegetables
are tender.
spicy tomato marinade Combine ingredients
in large bowl.
serve with a green salad.

note Soak bamboo skewers in cold water for at least
30 minutes before using to prevent splintering and
scorching during cooking.

VEGIES

pumpkin and haloumi salad

VEGETABLE AND PASTA SALAD WITH SUN-DRIED TOMATO MAYONNAISE

prep & cook time **30 minutes** serves **4**
nutritional count per serving **15.6g total fat**
(2g saturated fat); 2286kJ (547 cal);
79.8g carbohydrate; 16.8g protein; 9.1g fibre

375g penne pasta
5 yellow patty-pan squash (150g),
    halved crossways
2 medium zucchini (240g), sliced thinly
350g asparagus, trimmed, cut into
    5cm lengths
2 baby eggplants (120g), sliced thinly
1 small red onion (100g), cut into wedges
250g cherry tomatoes
1 medium red capsicum (200g), sliced thickly
½ cup (150g) mayonnaise
1 tablespoon sun-dried tomato pesto

1 Cook pasta in large saucepan of boiling water until just tender; drain.
2 Meanwhile, cook vegetables on heated oiled barbecue (or grill plate) until just tender.
3 Combine mayonnaise and pesto in large bowl. Add pasta and vegetables; toss gently.

PUMPKIN AND HALOUMI SALAD

prep & cook time **25 minutes** serves **4**
nutritional count per serving **27.3g total fat**
(9.6g saturated fat); 1639kJ (392 cal);
12.9g carbohydrate; 21.4g protein; 5.9g fibre

650g pumpkin, cut into thin wedges
200g green beans, halved
2 tablespoons olive oil
2 tablespoons red wine vinegar
¾ cup loosely packed fresh coriander leaves
¾ cup loosely packed fresh flat-leaf
    parsley leaves
100g baby spinach leaves
⅓ cup (65g) toasted pepitas
250g haloumi cheese, sliced thickly

1 Boil, steam or microwave pumpkin and beans, separately, until almost tender; drain. Rinse under cold water; drain. Place pumpkin on heated oiled barbecue (or grill plate); cook until tender.
2 Place oil, vinegar, coriander, parsley, spinach and pepitas in large bowl; toss gently.
3 Cook cheese on heated oiled barbecue until browned both sides. Add cheese, pumpkin and beans to bowl with spinach mix; toss gently.

vegetable and pasta salad with sun-dried tomato mayonnaise

mushroom burgers with the lot

MUSHROOM BURGERS WITH THE LOT

prep & cook time **20 minutes** serves **4**
nutritional count per serving **12.2g total fat**
(2.5g saturated fat); 1300kJ (311 cal);
30.9g carbohydrate; 16.4g protein; 6g fibre

50g baby spinach leaves
1 tablespoon lemon juice
1 tablespoon olive oil
1 teaspoon dijon mustard
4 thick slices ciabatta bread (200g)
1 large brown onion (200g), cut into 4 slices
4 large flat mushrooms (320g), halved
1 large tomato (220g), cut into 4 slices
4 eggs

1 Place spinach and combined juice, oil and mustard in medium bowl; toss gently.
2 Toast ciabatta, both sides, on heated oiled barbecue (or grill plate); cook onion, mushrooms and tomato on heated oiled barbecue until vegetables are just tender.
3 Meanwhile, cook eggs in lightly oiled egg rings on heated oiled barbecue flat plate until cooked as desired.
4 Divide ciabatta among serving plates; layer with mushroom, onion, tomato, egg and spinach mixture.

note In Italian, ciabatta means 'slipper', which is the traditional shape of this popular crisp-crusted wood-fired white bread. You can substitute it with turkish bread or focaccia.

VEGETABLE AND COUSCOUS SALAD

prep & cook time **20 minutes** serves **4**
nutritional count per serving **1.8g total fat**
(0.3g saturated fat); 1714kJ (410 cal);
79.8g carbohydrate; 14.6g protein; 5.9g fibre

1 medium kumara (400g), cut into
**   5mm slices**
2 large zucchini (300g), cut into 5mm slices
1½ cups (300g) couscous
1½ cups (375ml) hot chicken stock
450g can whole baby beetroot,
**   drained, quartered**

vegetable and couscous salad

40g baby spinach leaves
2 tablespoons coarsely chopped fresh
**   flat-leaf parsley**
orange dressing
1 teaspoon finely grated orange rind
¼ cup (60ml) orange juice
2 tablespoons white wine vinegar
1 teaspoon dijon mustard

1 Cook kumara and zucchini, in batches, on heated oiled barbecue (or grill plate), until tender. Cool 10 minutes.
2 Combine couscous with stock in large heatproof bowl, cover; stand 5 minutes or until liquid is absorbed, fluffing with fork occasionally.
3 Make orange dressing.
4 Add kumara, zucchini, beetroot, spinach and parsley to couscous; mix gently. Serve salad drizzled with orange dressing.
orange dressing Combine ingredients in screw-top jar; shake well.

note **Kumara** is the Polynesian name of an orange-fleshed sweet potato, often confused with yam. It is available from supermarkets.

eggplant, fetta and capsicum stack
with mesclun salad

EGGPLANT, FETTA AND CAPSICUM STACK WITH MESCLUN SALAD

prep & cook time **30 minutes** serves **4**
nutritional count per serving **29g total fat**
(9.9g saturated fat); 1822kJ (436 cal);
23g carbohydrate; 16.3g protein; 10.1g fibre

2 medium red capsicums (400g)
¼ cup (60ml) olive oil
2 tablespoons lemon juice
1 clove garlic, crushed
1 large eggplant (500g)
1 cup (150g) drained sun-dried tomatoes,
    chopped coarsely
¼ cup (40g) seeded kalamata olives,
    chopped coarsely
½ cup loosely packed fresh basil, torn
100g mesclun
2 tablespoons red wine vinegar
200g fetta cheese, cut into 8 slices
1 tablespoon small whole fresh basil leaves

1 Quarter capsicums; discard seeds and
membranes. Cook capsicum on heated oiled
barbecue (or grill plate), skin-side down, until
skin blisters and blackens. Cover with plastic
wrap for 5 minutes; peel away skin.

2 Meanwhile, combine 2 tablespoons of the oil
in small bowl with juice and garlic. Cut eggplant
lengthways into 8 slices; brush slices, both
sides, with oil mixture. Cook eggplant on heated
oiled barbecue, brushing occasionally with oil
mixture, until just tender.
3 Combine tomato, olives and basil in small
bowl. Place mesclun in medium bowl, drizzle
with vinegar and remaining oil; toss gently.
4 Place 1 slice of eggplant on each plate;
top each with 2 slices of cheese, 2 pieces of
capsicum and 1 remaining eggplant slice. Top
with tomato mixture, sprinkle with extra basil
leaves; serve with salad.

FENNEL, ASPARAGUS AND WALNUT SALAD

prep & cook time **30 minutes** serves **4**
nutritional count per serving **27.5g total fat**
(2.3g saturated fat); 1601kJ (383 cal);
21g carbohydrate; 8.6g protein; 10.4g fibre

6 small fennel bulbs (1.2kg), halved
    lengthways
750g asparagus, trimmed
1 tablespoon olive oil
¼ cup (60ml) walnut oil
2 teaspoons white sugar
¼ cup (60ml) lemon juice
2 nashi (400g), cored
1 tablespoon finely chopped fresh
    flat-leaf parsley
½ cup (50g) roasted walnuts,
    chopped coarsely

1 Cook fennel and asparagus on heated oiled
barbecue (or grill plate), brushing with olive oil,
until vegetables are just tender.
2 Meanwhile, whisk walnut oil, sugar and juice
in large bowl.
3 Cut nashi into thin wedges. Add fennel, nashi,
parsley and nuts to dressing; toss gently.
4 Divide asparagus among serving plates; top
with salad.

fennel, asparagus and walnut salad

grilled asian vegetables

GRILLED ASIAN VEGETABLES

prep & cook time 20 minutes serves 4
nutritional count per serving 10.7g total fat
(1.8g saturated fat); 811kJ (194 cal);
13.4g carbohydrate; 6.5g protein; 6.1g fibre

400g baby buk choy, trimmed, halved
    lengthways
2 tablespoons peanut oil
175g broccolini, halved
100g snow peas, trimmed
200g fresh baby corn, halved lengthways
2 tablespoons mirin
1 tablespoon vegetarian oyster sauce
1 tablespoon light soy sauce
1 clove garlic, crushed
1 teaspoon white sugar
½ teaspoon sesame oil

1 Boil, steam or microwave buk choy until
wilted; drain. Brush with half the peanut oil;
cook on heated oiled barbecue flat plate (or
grill plate) until tender.
2 Combine broccolini, peas and corn in large
bowl with remaining peanut oil; mix well. Cook
vegetables, in batches, on flat plate until tender.
3 Meanwhile, combine mirin, sauces, garlic,
sugar and sesame oil in same bowl; add
vegetables, mix well.

note **Vegetarian oyster sauce is made from blended
mushrooms and soy, and is available from health-food
stores and some supermarkets.**

MARINATED MIXED MUSHROOMS

prep & cook time 25 minutes (+ refrigeration) serves 4
nutritional count per serving 9.8g total fat
(1.7g saturated fat); 890kJ (213 cal);
14.9g carbohydrate; 9.2g protein; 7.7g fibre

2 cloves garlic, crushed
4cm piece fresh ginger (20g), grated
⅓ cup (80ml) light soy sauce
2 tablespoons mirin
2 tablespoons sake
2 tablespoons peanut oil
1 tablespoon white sugar
200g oyster mushrooms
200g shiitake mushrooms

marinated mixed mushrooms

200g button mushrooms
200g swiss brown mushrooms
200g enoki mushrooms
4 green onions, sliced diagonally

1 Combine garlic, ginger, sauce, mirin, sake,
oil and sugar in large bowl; add mushrooms,
mix gently. Cover; refrigerate 2 hours.
2 Drain mushrooms; reserve marinade in bowl.
3 Cook mushrooms, in batches, on heated oiled
barbecue flat plate (or grill plate) until tender.
4 Combine mushrooms and onion in bowl with
reserved marinade.

GRILLED TUNA WITH JAPANESE CHILLED SOBA SALAD

prep & cook time 30 minutes (+ refrigeration) serves 4
nutritional count per serving 11.9g total fat
(4.3g saturated fat); 2207kJ (528 cal);
45.1g carbohydrate; 52.1g protein; 2.8g fibre

250g soba noodles
¼ cup (70g) pickled pink ginger, sliced thinly
4 green onions, sliced thinly
4 x 175g tuna steaks
1 sheet toasted nori, shredded
soy mirin dressing
¼ cup (60ml) light soy sauce
⅓ cup (80ml) mirin
1 tablespoon rice vinegar
2 tablespoons cooking sake
1 teaspoon sesame oil
1 teaspoon wasabi paste

1 Cook noodles in large saucepan of boiling water until tender; drain. Rinse under cold water, drain. Cool.
2 Make soy mirin dressing.
3 Combine noodles, ginger and onion in large bowl, add three-quarters of the dressing; mix gently. Cover; refrigerate until chilled.
4 Cook tuna, both sides, on heated oiled barbecue (or grill plate) until just cooked (do not overcook or tuna will dry out).
5 Serve tuna drizzled with remaining dressing; top with nori. Serve with soba salad.
soy mirin dressing Combine ingredients in screw-top jar; shake well.

SEAFOOD

barbecued prawns with chilli lime dressing

BARBECUED SQUID SKEWERS WITH CHILLI DIPPING SAUCE

prep & cook time **30 minutes** makes **48**
nutritional count per skewer **3.7g total fat**
(0.8g saturated fat); 288kJ (69 cal);
1.5g carbohydrate; 7.2g protein; 0.4g fibre

8 cleaned baby squid hoods (500g)
2 tablespoons sweet chilli sauce
2 teaspoons finely grated lime rind
2 tablespoons peanut oil
chilli dipping sauce
2 tablespoons sweet chilli sauce
2 tablespoons lime juice
1 tablespoon fish sauce
1 fresh small red thai chilli, chopped finely
1 tablespoon finely chopped fresh coriander

1 Make chilli dipping sauce.
2 Cut squid hoods down centre to open out; score inside in diagonal pattern. Halve hoods lengthways; cut each piece into three strips. Thread one strip onto each skewer; place, in single layer, in large shallow dish.
3 Combine sauce, rind and oil in small bowl; pour over squid. Cook squid on heated oiled barbecue (or grill plate).
4 Serve skewers with chilli dipping sauce; sprinkle with coriander leaves.
chilli dipping sauce Combine ingredients in screw-top jar; shake well.

note **You need to soak 48 bamboo skewers for at least 30 minutes prior to using to prevent them from burning during cooking.**

BARBECUED PRAWNS WITH CHILLI LIME DRESSING

prep & cook time **35 minutes** serves **4**
nutritional count per serving **29.8g total fat**
(4.2g saturated fat); 1914kJ (458 cal);
3.4g carbohydrate; 44.1g protein; 0.4g fibre

1.7kg uncooked large king prawns
¼ cup coarsely chopped fresh coriander
chilli lime dressing
⅓ cup (80ml) lime juice
⅓ cup (80ml) lemon juice
½ cup (125ml) olive oil
2 cloves garlic, crushed
2 teaspoons caster sugar
2 teaspoons sea salt flakes
3 fresh long red chillies, sliced thinly

1 Make chilli lime dressing.
2 Devein prawns leaving heads and shells intact. Combine prawns in large bowl with half the dressing; cook prawns on heated oiled barbecue (or grill plate).
3 Stir coriander into remaining dressing; serve with prawns. Serve with a green salad.
chilli lime dressing Combine ingredients in small bowl.

barbecued squid skewers with chilli dipping sauce

grilled fish with thai-style dressing

GRILLED FISH WITH THAI-STYLE DRESSING

prep & cook time **25 minutes** serves **4**
nutritional count per serving **4.7g total fat**
(1.4g saturated fat); 1074kJ (257 cal);
9.3g carbohydrate; 42.9g protein; 1.9g fibre

4 x 200g firm white fish fillets
⅓ cup (80ml) lime juice
2 tablespoons grated palm sugar
1 tablespoon fish sauce
100g snow pea sprouts
1 cup loosely packed fresh mint leaves
½ cup loosely packed fresh coriander leaves
3 shallots (75g), sliced thinly
2 fresh long red chillies, sliced thinly

1 Cook fish on heated oiled barbecue (or grill plate).
2 Meanwhile, combine juice, sugar and sauce in small bowl.
3 Combine sprouts, mint, coriander, shallots and chilli in medium bowl.
4 Serve fish with salad; drizzle with dressing.

note You can use any firm white fish fillet, for example, ling or blue-eye, in this recipe.

KAFFIR LIME AND LEMON GRASS GRILLED TROUT

prep & cook time **1 hour** serves **6**
nutritional count per serving **14.3g total fat**
(3g saturated fat); 1262kJ (302 cal);
1.2g carbohydrate; 41.4g protein; 0.7g fibre

10cm stick fresh lemon grass (20g), chopped coarsely
4cm piece fresh ginger (20g), sliced thickly
2 cloves garlic, quartered
2 tablespoons peanut oil
1 tablespoon sweet chilli sauce
1 tablespoon lime juice
2 green onions, chopped finely
1 whole ocean trout (2.4kg)
1 lime, peeled, sliced thinly
10cm stick fresh lemon grass (20g), sliced diagonally

kaffir lime and lemon grass grilled trout

1 kaffir lime leaf, shredded thinly
⅓ cup loosely packed fresh coriander leaves
1 lime, cut into wedges

1 Process chopped lemon grass, ginger, garlic, oil, sauce and juice until smooth. Stir in onion.
2 Place long piece of baking paper on bench; place fish on paper. Fill cavity with lemon grass mixture. Score fish three times on both sides through thickest part of flesh; cover cuts with lime slices. Sprinkle fish with sliced lemon grass and lime leaf. Fold paper over to completely enclose fish then wrap fish tightly in foil.
3 Cook fish on heated oiled barbecue (or grill plate) for 25 minutes; turn, cook a further 20 minutes or until cooked through.
4 Serve fish sprinkled with coriander; accompany with lime wedges.

thai fish burgers

2 Cook patties on heated oiled barbecue flat plate about 15 minutes or until cooked through.
3 Meanwhile, combine juice, sugar and extra sauce in medium bowl; toss through spinach and cucumber.
4 Split buns in half; toast cut-sides. Sandwich salad, patties and sweet chilli sauce between bun halves.

note We used blue-eye here, but any firm white fish fillets can be used.

THAI FISH BURGERS

prep & cook time 35 minutes serves 4
nutritional count per serving 5.3g total fat
(0.7g saturated fat); 1722kJ (412 cal);
55.2g carbohydrate; 32g protein; 5.7g fibre

500g blue-eye fillets, chopped coarsely
1 tablespoon fish sauce
1 tablespoon kecap manis
1 clove garlic, quartered
1 fresh small red thai chilli, chopped coarsely
50g green beans, trimmed, chopped coarsely
¼ cup (20g) fried shallots
¼ cup coarsely chopped fresh coriander
1 tablespoon lime juice
2 teaspoons brown sugar
2 teaspoons fish sauce, extra
60g baby spinach leaves
1 lebanese cucumber (130g), seeded, sliced thinly
4 hamburger buns (360g)
⅓ cup (80ml) sweet chilli sauce

1 Blend or process fish fillets, fish sauce, kecap manis, garlic and chilli until smooth. Combine fish mixture in large bowl with beans, shallots and coriander; shape into four patties.

LOBSTER TAILS WITH LIME BUTTER AND PINEAPPLE MINT SALSA

prep & cook time 30 minutes serves 4
nutritional count per serving 21.9g total fat
(13.8g saturated fat); 1538kJ (368 cal);
10.1g carbohydrate; 31.1g protein; 3.1g fibre

100g butter
1 teaspoon finely grated lime rind
1 fresh small red thai chilli, chopped finely
2cm piece fresh ginger (10g), grated
4 uncooked small lobster tails in shells (660g)
pineapple mint salsa
1 small pineapple (900g), chopped coarsely
2 tablespoons lime juice
½ cup finely chopped fresh mint
1 fresh long red chilli, chopped finely

1 Make pineapple mint salsa.
2 Melt butter in small saucepan; cook rind, chilli and ginger, stirring, 2 minutes.
3 Using scissors, cut soft shell from underneath lobster tails to expose meat; cut lobster tails in half lengthways. Brush with butter mixture; cook, in batches, on heated oiled barbecue (or grill plate) until cooked through. Serve with salsa.
pineapple mint salsa Combine ingredients in medium bowl.

lobster tails with lime butter and pineapple mint salsa

TIKKA PRAWNS WITH RAITA

prep & cook time **30 minutes** serves **6**

Shell and devein 24 uncooked large prawns, leaving tails intact. Cook prawns, in batches, on heated oiled barbecue, brushing with combined ¼ cup tikka paste and ¾ cup yogurt, until prawns are just cooked through. Combine extra ¾ cup yogurt with ¼ cup chopped fresh coriander and ½ teaspoon ground cumin; serve with prawns.

PRAWN AND GREEN ONION SKEWERS

prep & cook time **35 minutes** serves **4**

Shell and devein 1.5kg uncooked large prawns leaving the tails intact. Combine prawns in medium bowl with 2 tablespoons lemon juice, 1 tablespoon olive oil and 2 cloves crushed garlic. Cut 12 green onions into 4cm lengths. Thread prawns and onion onto skewers. Cook skewers on heated oiled barbecue until changed in colour and just cooked through.

FAST PRAWNS

SPICY PRAWNS

prep & cook time **25 minutes** serves **6**

Shell and devein 18 uncooked large prawns,
leaving tails intact. Combine 2 cloves crushed
garlic, 1 finely chopped fresh long red chilli and
2 tablespoons olive oil in large bowl; add prawns.
Cook prawns, in batches, on heated oiled
barbecue until just cooked through. Serve
prawns drizzled with lemon juice.

BARBECUED PRAWNS

prep & cook time **30 minutes** serves **4**

Remove heads and legs from 20 uncooked
large prawns; devein prawns, leaving tails and
shells intact. Process 1 coarsely chopped
medium onion, ½ cup yogurt, ½ teaspoon
ground turmeric, ½ teaspoon chilli powder,
1 tablespoon sweet paprika, 1 teaspoon grated
fresh ginger, 2 cloves crushed garlic and
1 tablespoon lemon juice until smooth. Reserve
a quarter of the mixture; combine remaining
yogurt mixture with prawns. Cook prawns
on heated oiled barbecue until just cooked
through, brushing occasionally with reserved
yogurt mixture during cooking.

SUMAC CHICKEN WITH MINTED EGGPLANT

prep & cook time 25 minutes **serves** 4
nutritional count per serving 28.3g total fat
(5.7g saturated fat); 2107kJ (504 cal);
14.2g carbohydrate; 45.9g protein; 5.1g fibre

1 teaspoon finely grated lemon rind
⅓ cup (80ml) lemon juice
2 teaspoons sumac
2 teaspoons caster sugar
1 tablespoon tahini
800g chicken tenderloins
2 medium eggplants (600g), sliced thickly
¼ cup (60ml) olive oil
½ cup coarsely chopped fresh mint
1 medium lemon (140g), sliced thickly

1 Combine rind, half the juice, sumac, sugar,
tahini and chicken in large bowl.
2 Cook chicken on heated oiled barbecue
(or grill plate) until cooked through. Cover to
keep warm.
3 Cook eggplant on cleaned heated oiled
barbecue until browned; combine eggplant in
medium bowl with remaining juice, oil and mint.
4 Serve chicken and eggplant with lemon.

note Tahini is a sesame seed paste available from
health-food stores and many supermarkets.

POULTRY

mixed satay sticks

MIXED SATAY STICKS

prep & cook time **35 minutes (+ refrigeration)** serves **4**
nutritional count per serving **41.7g total fat**
(15.5g saturated fat); 2500kJ (598 cal);
9.2g carbohydrate; 45.5g protein; 3.7g fibre

250g chicken breast fillets
250g beef eye fillet
250g pork fillet
2 cloves garlic, crushed
2 teaspoons brown sugar
¼ teaspoon sambal oelek
1 teaspoon ground turmeric
¼ teaspoon curry powder
½ teaspoon ground cumin
½ teaspoon ground coriander
2 tablespoons peanut oil
satay sauce
½ cup (70g) roasted unsalted peanuts
2 tablespoons red curry paste
¾ cup (180ml) coconut milk
¼ cup (60ml) chicken stock
1 tablespoon lime juice
1 tablespoon brown sugar

1 Cut chicken, beef and pork into long 1.5cm-thick strips; thread strips onto skewers. Place skewers, in single layer, on tray or in shallow baking dish; brush with combined garlic, sugar, sambal, spices and oil. Cover; refrigerate 3 hours.
2 Make satay sauce.
3 Cook skewers on heated oiled barbecue (or grill plate) until browned all over and cooked as desired. Serve immediately with satay sauce.
satay sauce Process nuts until chopped finely; add paste, process until just combined. Bring coconut milk to the boil in small saucepan; add peanut mixture, whisking until smooth. Reduce heat, add stock; cook, stirring, about 3 minutes or until sauce thickens slightly. Add juice and sugar, stirring, until sugar has dissolved.

note Soak 12 bamboo skewers in cold water for at least 30 minutes before using to prevent them from burning during cooking.

TAMARIND, ORANGE AND HONEY DRUMETTES

prep & cook time **45 minutes (+ refrigeration)** serves **6**
nutritional count per serving **22.3g total fat**
(6.3g saturated fat); 1994kJ (477 cal);
30.8g carbohydrate; 37g protein; 4.1g fibre

2 teaspoons finely grated orange rind
⅓ cup (80ml) orange juice
⅓ cup (115g) honey
⅓ cup (100g) tamarind concentrate
½ cup (125ml) japanese soy sauce
30 chicken drumettes (2kg)
600g baby buk choy, trimmed, quartered
2 medium red capsicums (400g), sliced thickly
230g fresh baby corn
1 tablespoon tamarind concentrate, extra
2 teaspoons sesame oil

1 Combine rind, juice, honey, tamarind and half the sauce in large bowl, add chicken; turn to coat in marinade. Cover; refrigerate 3 hours.
2 Cook chicken on heated oiled barbecue (or grill plate), turning and brushing occasionally with marinade, about 30 minutes or until cooked.
3 Meanwhile, cook buk choy, capsicum and corn on heated oiled barbecue flat plate until tender. Place vegetables in medium bowl with combined remaining sauce, extra tamarind and oil; toss to combine. Serve with chicken.

tamarind, orange and honey drumettes

pesto chicken with grilled zucchini

PESTO CHICKEN WITH GRILLED ZUCCHINI

prep & cook time **25 minutes** serves **4**
nutritional count per serving **33.1g total fat**
(7.6g saturated fat); 2611kJ (481 cal);
3.3g carbohydrate; 41.7g protein; 3.6g fibre

6 medium zucchini (720g), sliced thickly
    lengthways
2 tablespoons olive oil
1 clove garlic, crushed
1 tablespoon finely chopped fresh basil
1 teaspoon finely grated lemon rind
⅓ cup (90g) sun-dried tomato pesto
2 tablespoons chicken stock
4 x 200g chicken thigh fillets, cut into thirds

1 Cook zucchini on heated oiled barbecue (or
grill plate), in batches, until tender. Combine
with oil, garlic, basil and rind in medium bowl;
cover to keep warm.
2 Combine pesto, stock and chicken in large
bowl. Cook chicken on heated oiled barbecue,
brushing occasionally with pesto mixture, until
cooked. Serve chicken with zucchini.
serve with **rocket leaves.**

GRILLED CHICKEN WITH GREEN OLIVE BUTTER

prep & cook time **35 minutes** serves **4**
nutritional count per serving **32g total fat**
(17g saturated fat); 2316kJ (554 cal);
18.6g carbohydrate; 46.5g protein; 3.5g fibre

400g baby new potatoes, sliced thickly
800g chicken breast fillets
150g baby spinach leaves
green olive butter
100g butter, softened
¾ cup (90g) seeded green olives,
    chopped coarsely
1 teaspoon finely grated lemon rind
1 clove garlic, crushed
1 tablespoon coarsely chopped fresh basil

1 Make green olive butter.
2 Boil, steam or microwave potato until tender;
drain. Cover to keep warm.
3 Meanwhile, halve chicken fillets horizontally.

grilled chicken with green olive butter

Cook chicken on heated oiled barbecue (or
grill plate) until cooked through.
4 Divide potato among plates; top with spinach,
chicken then green olive butter.
green olive butter Combine ingredients in
small bowl.

sichuan duck with snow pea and watercress salad

SICHUAN DUCK WITH SNOW PEA AND WATERCRESS SALAD

prep & cook time **1 hour (+ refrigeration)** serves **4**
nutritional count per serving **92.9g total fat
(25.6g saturated fat); 4314kJ (1032 cal);
6.5g carbohydrate; 35.1g protein; 4.1g fibre**

½ cup (125ml) chinese cooking wine
2 tablespoons light soy sauce
2 cloves garlic, crushed
4cm piece fresh ginger (20g), sliced thinly
1 teaspoon sesame oil
4 duck marylands (1.2kg)
2 teaspoons sichuan peppercorns
1 teaspoon sea salt
100g watercress, trimmed
150g snow peas, trimmed, sliced thinly
1 small red onion (100g), sliced thinly
½ cup loosely packed fresh coriander leaves
½ cup (70g) roasted unsalted peanuts,
    chopped coarsely
2 tablespoons lime juice
1 tablespoon peanut oil
1 clove garlic, crushed, extra

1 Combine wine, sauce, garlic, ginger and sesame oil in large bowl with duck. Cover; refrigerate 3 hours or overnight. Drain duck; discard marinade.
2 Dry-fry peppercorns in small frying pan until fragrant. Crush peppercorns and salt using mortar and pestle; press mixture onto duck skin.
3 Cook duck on heated oiled barbecue (or grill plate) about 40 minutes or until cooked, turning halfway through cooking time.
4 Meanwhile, combine remaining ingredients in large bowl; serve with duck.

GRILLED CHICKEN WITH CORIANDER AND CHILLI

prep & cook time **35 minutes (+ refrigeration)** serves **4**
nutritional count per serving **29.5g total fat
(7.8g saturated fat); 2094kJ (501 cal);
5.2g carbohydrate; 53.5g protein; 1.7g fibre**

8 chicken thigh cutlets (1.6kg)
coriander and chilli paste
2 teaspoons coriander seeds
4 fresh small red thai chillies,
    chopped coarsely
1 teaspoon ground cumin
2 whole cloves
2 cardamom pods, bruised
¼ teaspoon ground turmeric
10cm stick fresh lemon grass (20g),
    chopped coarsely
2 medium brown onions (300g),
    chopped coarsely
4 cloves garlic
⅓ cup (80ml) lime juice
2 teaspoons coarse cooking salt
2 tablespoons peanut oil

1 Make coriander and chilli paste.
2 Pierce chicken all over with sharp knife. Combine paste and chicken in large bowl, rubbing paste into cuts. Cover; refrigerate 3 hours or overnight.
3 Cook chicken, covered, on heated oiled barbecue (or grill plate), 5 minutes. Uncover; cook, turning occasionally, about 20 minutes or until cooked.
coriander and chilli paste Blend or process ingredients until mixture forms a smooth paste.
serve with **lime wedges and thin rice noodles.**

grilled chicken with coriander and chilli

honey, soy and sesame chicken wings

HONEY, SOY AND SESAME CHICKEN WINGS

prep & cook time **45 minutes (+ refrigeration)** serves **4**
nutritional count per serving **10.3g total fat**
(3g saturated fat); 1233kJ (295 cal);
12.6g carbohydrate; 37.4g protein; 0.4g fibre

1kg chicken wings
¼ cup (60ml) japanese soy sauce
2 tablespoons honey
1 clove garlic, crushed
2cm piece fresh ginger (10g), grated
2 teaspoons sesame seeds
1 teaspoon sesame oil

1 Cut chicken wings into three pieces at joints; discard tips. Combine sauce, honey, garlic, ginger, seeds and oil in large bowl with chicken. Cover; refrigerate 3 hours or overnight.
2 Cook chicken on heated oiled barbecue (or grill plate), turning and basting occasionally with marinade, about 30 minutes or until cooked.

chicken yakitori with sesame dipping sauce

CHICKEN YAKITORI WITH SESAME DIPPING SAUCE

prep & cook time **30 minutes** serves **4**
nutritional count per serving **20.4g total fat**
(6.4g saturated fat); 1643kJ (393 cal);
3.8g carbohydrate; 47.1g protein; 0.1g fibre

12 chicken tenderloins (1kg)
sesame dipping sauce
¼ cup (60ml) light soy sauce
2 tablespoons mirin
3 teaspoons white sugar
½ teaspoon sesame oil
1 teaspoon sesame seeds

1 Make sesame dipping sauce.
2 Thread each tenderloin onto a skewer; brush skewers with half the dipping sauce. Cook skewers, in batches, on heated oiled barbecue (or grill plate) until chicken is cooked. Serve skewers with remaining dipping sauce.
sesame dipping sauce Combine ingredients in small saucepan; stir over medium heat until sugar dissolves.

note Soak 12 bamboo skewers in cold water for at least 30 minutes to prevent burning during cooking.

sesame wasabi chicken with daikon salad

SESAME WASABI CHICKEN WITH DAIKON SALAD

prep & cook time **1 hour** serves **4**
nutritional count per serving **31.3g total fat**
(7.7g saturated fat); 1948kJ (466 cal);
7.2g carbohydrate; 36.5g protein; 4.1g fibre

1 tablespoon japanese soy sauce
1 tablespoon sesame oil
2 tablespoons wasabi paste
8 chicken drumsticks (1.2kg)
daikon salad
2 medium carrots (240g)
1 small daikon (400g)
6 green onions, sliced thinly
1 tablespoon mirin
1 tablespoon lime juice
2 teaspoons sesame oil
2 teaspoons japanese soy sauce
2 tablespoons roasted sesame seeds

1 Combine sauce, oil, wasabi and chicken in large bowl; turn to coat chicken in mixture. Cook chicken on heated oiled barbecue (or grill plate), brushing occasionally with marinade, about 40 minutes or until cooked through.

2 Make daikon salad. Serve chicken with salad.
daikon salad Using vegetable peeler, slice carrots and daikon into ribbons. Place in large bowl with remaining ingredients; toss to combine.

INDOCHINE GRILLED CHICKEN SALAD

prep & cook time **1 hour (+ refrigeration)** serves **4**
nutritional count per serving **20.5g total fat**
(6.6g saturated fat); 1668kJ (399 cal);
17.2g carbohydrate; 26.9g protein; 4.2g fibre

2 teaspoons five-spice powder
¼ cup (60ml) mirin
2 tablespoons chinese cooking wine
2 cloves garlic, crushed
4 x 200g chicken thigh cutlets
125g rice vermicelli
150g snow peas, sliced thinly
1 cup (80g) bean sprouts
2 green onions, sliced thinly
½ cup coarsely chopped fresh coriander
¼ cup loosely packed vietnamese mint leaves
2 medium carrots (240g), cut into matchsticks
lime dressing
⅓ cup (80ml) lime juice
⅓ cup (80ml) mirin
2 cloves garlic, crushed
1 tablespoon grated palm sugar

1 Combine five-spice, mirin, wine, garlic and chicken in large bowl; turn to coat chicken in marinade. Cover; refrigerate 3 hours or overnight.
2 Make lime dressing.
3 Cook chicken on heated oiled barbecue (or grill plate), turning and brushing occasionally with marinade, about 40 minutes or until cooked.
4 Meanwhile, place vermicelli in large heatproof bowl, cover with boiling water; stand until just tender, drain. Rinse under cold water; drain.
5 Place vermicelli and dressing in large bowl with remaining ingredients, toss salad to combine. Serve with chicken.
lime dressing Combine ingredients in screw-top jar; shake well.

indochine grilled chicken salad

CHICKEN TIKKA WITH CUCUMBER MINT RAITA

prep & cook time **20 minutes** serves **4**

Brush 4 chicken breast fillets with 2 tablespoons tikka paste. Cook chicken on heated oiled barbecue (or grill plate) until browned and cooked through. Serve with combined ½ cup yogurt, 1 small peeled, seeded and finely chopped lebanese cucumber, 1 tablespoon finely chopped fresh mint and a pinch of ground cumin.

CHICKEN WITH MUSTARD AND ROSEMARY

prep & cook time **25 minutes** serves **4**

Combine 4 chicken breast fillets with 1 crushed garlic clove, 1 tablespoon wholegrain mustard, 2 tablespoons lemon juice, 1 tablespoon olive oil and 1 tablespoon finely chopped fresh rosemary; stand 10 minutes. Cook chicken on heated oiled barbecue (or grill plate) until browned and cooked through.

FAST CHICKEN

BARBECUED THAI CHICKEN

prep & cook time **20 minutes** serves **4**

Combine 4 chicken thigh fillets with ⅓ cup sweet chilli sauce, 1 crushed garlic clove, 1 tablespoon fish sauce, 1 tablespoon brown sugar and 2 teaspoons finely chopped fresh lemon grass. Cook chicken on heated oiled barbecue (or grill plate) until browned and cooked through.

BARBECUED CHICKEN WITH GARLIC AND CAPER BUTTER

prep & cook time **20 minutes** serves **4**

Melt 60g butter in small saucepan; add 1 crushed garlic clove, 1 tablespoon rinsed, drained capers and 2 teaspoons finely chopped fresh oregano. Cook 500g chicken tenderloins on heated oiled barbecue (or grill plate) until browned on one side. Turn tenderloins; spoon over half the butter mixture. Cook until chicken is just cooked through. Serve with remaining butter mixture.

HERBED RIB-EYE WITH TAPENADE MASH

prep & cook time 35 minutes serves 4
nutritional count per serving 34g total fat
(14.3g saturated fat); 2930kJ (761 cal);
41.1g carbohydrate; 54.6g protein; 6.4g fibre

4 large potatoes (1.2kg), chopped coarsely
1 tablespoon dried italian herbs
1 clove garlic, crushed
2 tablespoons olive oil
4 x 200g beef rib-eye steaks
½ cup (125ml) cream
2 tablespoons black olive tapenade
60g baby rocket leaves

1 Boil, steam or microwave potato until tender;
drain. Cover to keep warm.
2 Meanwhile, combine herbs, garlic, oil and
beef in medium bowl.
3 Cook beef on heated oiled barbecue (or grill
plate), brushing occasionally with herb mixture,
until cooked as desired. Remove from heat,
cover; stand 5 minutes.
4 Mash potato in large bowl with cream and
tapenade. Stir in half the rocket.
5 Serve beef with mash and remaining rocket.

note Tapenade is an olive paste made from a blend of
capers, olives, anchovies and olive oil. It is available
from supermarkets and delicatessens.

BEEF

beef and reef with kumara hash browns

BEEF AND REEF WITH KUMARA HASH BROWNS

prep & cook time **40 minutes** serves **4**
nutritional count per serving **22.5g total fat**
(11.1g saturated fat); 2383kJ (570 cal);
31.3g carbohydrate; 57.2g protein; 6.5g fibre

1 large kumara (500g), chopped coarsely
1 small brown onion (80g), chopped finely
2 tablespoons finely chopped fresh chives
1 egg yolk
16 uncooked medium king prawns (720g)
1 teaspoon salt
½ teaspoon cracked black pepper
½ teaspoon hot paprika
2 trimmed corn cobs (500g)
4 beef rib-eye steaks (800g)
garlic butter
50g butter, softened
2 cloves garlic, crushed
1 tablespoon finely chopped fresh chives

1 Boil, steam or microwave kumara until tender; drain. Mash kumara in medium bowl with onion, chives and egg yolk.
2 Meanwhile, shell and devein prawns leaving tails intact. Combine salt, pepper and paprika

in large bowl, add prawns; toss prawns to coat in mixture.
3 Cut corn in half crossways then in half lengthways. Cook steaks and corn on heated oiled barbecue (or grill plate) until steaks are cooked as desired and corn is tender. Cover to keep warm.
4 Shape kumara mixture into four patties. Cook patties on heated oiled flat plate, flattening with spatula, until browned both sides.
5 Make garlic butter.
6 Cook prawns on heated oiled barbecue until changed in colour.
7 Top steaks with prawns and butter. Serve with corn and hash browns.
garlic butter Combine ingredients in small bowl.

CHILLI AND HONEY BARBECUED STEAK WITH COLESLAW

prep & cook time **15 minutes** serves **4**
nutritional count per serving **15.2g total fat**
(5.4g saturated fat); 1605kJ (384 cal);
16.6g carbohydrate; 44g protein; 3.6g fibre

2 tablespoons barbecue sauce
1 tablespoon worcestershire sauce
1 tablespoon honey
1 fresh long red chilli, chopped finely
1 clove garlic, crushed
4 x 200g beef new-york cut steaks
coleslaw
2 tablespoons mayonnaise
1 tablespoon white wine vinegar
2 cups (160g) finely shredded white cabbage
1 cup (80g) finely shredded red cabbage
1 medium carrot (120g), grated coarsely
3 thinly sliced green onions

1 Combine sauces, honey, chilli, garlic and beef in large bowl; turn to coat beef in mixture.
2 Cook beef on heated oiled barbecue (or grill plate) until browned and cooked as desired.
3 Make coleslaw; serve with steaks.
coleslaw Place mayonnaise and vinegar in screw-top jar; shake well. Place dressing in large bowl with cabbages, carrot and onions; toss gently.

chilli and honey barbecued steak with coleslaw

beef teriyaki platter

BEEF TERIYAKI PLATTER

prep & cook time 30 minutes (+ refrigeration) serves 4
nutritional count per serving 9.3g total fat
(3.8g saturated fat); 1032kJ (247 cal);
3.5g carbohydrate; 36.1g protein; 2g fibre

⅓ cup (80ml) teriyaki sauce
3cm piece fresh ginger (15g), grated
1 clove garlic, crushed
3 x 200g new-york cut beef steaks, trimmed
500g asparagus, trimmed
8 green onions, trimmed
1 teaspoon wasabi paste
¼ cup (60ml) japanese soy sauce

1 Combine teriyaki sauce, ginger, garlic and
beef in large bowl. Cover; refrigerate 3 hours.
2 Cook beef on heated oiled barbecue (or grill
plate) until cooked as desired. Remove from
heat, cover; stand 5 minutes then slice thinly.
3 Cook asparagus and onion on heated oiled
barbecue flat plate until tender.
4 Combine wasabi and soy sauce. Serve beef
with vegetables, accompany with sauce.

CANTONESE BEEF PATTIES WITH GRILLED GAI LAN

prep & cook time 45 minutes serves 4
nutritional count per serving 20.2g total fat
(6.8g saturated fat); 2077kJ (497 cal);
26.6g carbohydrate; 48g protein; 8.3g fibre

800g beef mince
1 medium brown onion (150g), chopped finely
3 cloves garlic, crushed
2cm piece fresh ginger (10g), grated
1 fresh small red thai chilli, chopped finely
227g can water chestnuts, drained, rinsed,
    chopped finely
¼ cup finely chopped fresh chives
1 egg
½ cup (35g) stale breadcrumbs
1 tablespoon hoisin sauce
1 tablespoon water
2 tablespoons oyster sauce
⅓ cup (80ml) hoisin sauce, extra
2 teaspoons sesame oil
1kg gai lan, chopped coarsely

cantonese beef patties with grilled gai lan

1 Combine beef, onion, two-thirds of the
garlic, ginger, chilli, chestnuts, chives, egg,
breadcrumbs and hoisin sauce in large bowl;
shape mixture into eight patties.
2 Combine the water, oyster sauce, extra
hoisin sauce and remaining garlic in small
bowl. Reserve ¼ cup hoisin mixture.
3 Brush patties with remaining hoisin mixture;
cook patties, both sides, on heated oiled
barbecue flat plate about 10 minutes or until
cooked as desired.
4 Heat sesame oil on flat plate; cook gai lan
until wilted. Serve gai lan topped with patties;
drizzle with reserved hoisin mixture.

note Hoisin is a sweet, thick Chinese barbecue sauce
made from salted fermented soya beans, onion and
garlic. It is used as a marinade or baste for stir-fried,
braised or roasted foods, and can be found in all Asian
food shops and most supermarkets.

4 Cook patties and eggplant, in batches, on heated oiled flat plate (or grill plate) until browned both sides and cooked through.
5 Halve bread pieces horizontally; toast cut-sides on heated barbecue. Spread cut-sides with yogurt mixture; sandwich rocket, eggplant and patties between toast.

CHEESE-STUFFED STEAKS WITH RADICCHIO SALAD

prep & cook time **40 minutes** serves 4
nutritional count per serving **48.1g total fat** (9.8g saturated fat); 2596kJ (621 cal); 12g carbohydrate; 34.2g protein; 5.4g fibre

4 x 125g beef eye-fillet steaks
80g brie cheese, sliced thickly into 4 pieces
1 small radicchio (150g), trimmed, quartered
1 cup (120g) pecans, roasted,
   chopped coarsely
1 large pear (330g), unpeeled, sliced thickly
1 cup loosely packed fresh flat-leaf
   parsley leaves
¼ cup (60ml) olive oil
2 tablespoons lemon juice

1 Slice steaks in half horizontally. Sandwich cheese slices between steak halves; tie with kitchen string to secure.
2 Cook steaks on heated oiled barbecue (or grill plate) until cooked through.
3 Meanwhile, cook radicchio on heated grill plate until browned lightly.
4 Combine radicchio with remaining ingredients in bowl; serve with steaks.

note We used a triple-cream brie cheese; you can replace it with the more easily found blue-vein variety, but choose one that's mild and very creamy.

beef burger with grilled eggplant and rocket

BEEF BURGER WITH GRILLED EGGPLANT AND ROCKET

prep & cook time **35 minutes** serves 4
nutritional count per serving **19.3g total fat** (6.4g saturated fat); 2546kJ (609 cal); 61.8g carbohydrate; 42.6g protein; 7.5g fibre

⅓ cup (95g) greek-style yogurt
⅓ cup (90g) hummus
1 medium eggplant (300g)
500g beef mince
2 cloves garlic, crushed
1 tablespoon tomato paste
1 small brown onion (80g), chopped finely
1 fresh small red thai chilli, chopped finely
½ cup coarsely chopped fresh basil
½ cup (35g) stale breadcrumbs
1 egg
1 loaf turkish bread (430g), cut into quarters
40g baby rocket leaves

1 Combine yogurt and hummus in small bowl.
2 Cut eggplant lengthways into 6 slices; discard two skin-side pieces.
3 Combine mince, garlic, paste, onion, chilli, basil, breadcrumbs and egg in large bowl; shape mixture into four patties.

cheese-stuffed steaks with radicchio salad

fennel-flavoured veal chops with garlic mustard butter

FENNEL-FLAVOURED VEAL CHOPS WITH GARLIC MUSTARD BUTTER

prep & cook time 25 minutes serves 4
nutritional count per serving 29.7g total fat
(13.2g saturated fat); 1831kJ (438 cal);
2.1g carbohydrate; 39.9g protein; 2.7g fibre

2 teaspoons fennel seeds
1 teaspoon sea salt
½ teaspoon cracked black pepper
2 tablespoons olive oil
4 x 200g veal chops
4 flat mushrooms (320g)
80g butter, softened
1 tablespoon coarsely chopped fresh
    flat-leaf parsley
1 clove garlic, crushed
1 tablespoon wholegrain mustard
80g baby rocket leaves

1 Using mortar and pestle, crush combined
seeds, salt and pepper coarsely; stir in oil.
Rub mixture all over veal.
2 Cook veal and mushrooms on heated oiled
barbecue (or grill plate) until browned both
sides and cooked as desired.
3 Meanwhile, combine butter, parsley, garlic
and mustard in small bowl.
4 Divide rocket among serving plates; top with
mushroom, veal then butter.

SPICED SLICED BEEF RUMP WITH CHILLI PEANUT SAUCE

prep & cook time 45 minutes serves 4
nutritional count per serving 35.6g total fat
(9.4g saturated fat); 3047kJ (729 cal);
41.1g carbohydrate; 58.6g protein; 5.4g fibre

1 fresh small red thai chilli, chopped finely
1 shallot (25g), chopped finely
1 tablespoon peanut oil
800g beef rump steak
¼ cup (60ml) water
⅓ cup (75g) caster sugar
¼ cup (60ml) fish sauce
½ cup (125ml) lime juice
1 medium carrot (120g), chopped finely

spiced sliced beef rump with chilli peanut sauce

1 medium red capsicum (200g),
    chopped finely
1 cup (140g) crushed roasted
    unsalted peanuts
20 peking duck pancakes (200g)

1 Combine chilli and shallot in medium bowl.
Combine half the chilli mixture with oil in large
bowl; add beef, turn to coat in mixture.
2 Cook beef on heated oiled barbecue (or grill
plate), turning once, until cooked. Cover; stand
5 minutes then slice thinly.
3 Meanwhile, stir the water, sugar, sauce,
juice, carrot, capsicum and nuts into remaining
chilli mixture.
4 Heat pancakes by folding each into quarters;
place in steamer over large saucepan of
simmering water until just pliable. Serve beef
with chilli peanut sauce and pancakes.

note Peking duck pancakes are small, crêpe-like
pancakes sold fresh, usually in containers holding
20, located in the refrigerated section of most Asian
grocery stores. Steam them for just a few minutes,
until they are warm and pliable.

HARISSA LAMB CUTLETS WITH CORN AND GARLIC

prep & cook time 30 minutes (+ refrigeration) **serves** 4
nutritional count per serving 49.4g total fat
(21.5g saturated fat); 3478kJ (832 cal);
52.3g carbohydrate; 36.3g protein; 18.4g fibre

¼ cup (75g) harissa paste
2 tablespoons olive oil
12 lamb cutlets (600g)
4 fresh corn cobs (1.5kg), husks on
4 bulbs garlic
harissa butter
3 teaspoons harissa paste
80g butter, softened

1 Combine harissa and oil in large bowl, add
lamb; toss lamb to coat in mixture. Cover;
refrigerate overnight.
2 Carefully pull husk down corn cob, leaving
it attached at the base. Remove as much silk
as possible then bring husk back over cob to
cover kernels. Tie each cob with kitchen string
to hold husk in place; soak corn overnight in
large bowl of water.
3 Make harissa butter. Spread 2 teaspoons of
the harissa butter over each garlic bulb; wrap
garlic bulbs individually in foil.
4 Drain corn. Cook corn and garlic parcels
on heated oiled barbecue (or grill plate) about
15 minutes or until corn is cooked as desired
and garlic is tender.
5 Meanwhile, cook lamb on heated oiled
barbecue until cooked as desired.
6 Spread corn with remaining harissa butter;
serve with lamb and garlic.
harissa butter Combine ingredients in
small bowl.

LAMB

tandoori lamb with fresh melon and coconut chutney

SPICED LAMB BURGER WITH TZATZIKI

prep & cook time **30 minutes** serves **4**
nutritional count per serving **21.1g total fat**
(7.5g saturated fat); 2604kJ (623 cal);
60g carbohydrate; 43.8g protein; 8g fibre

500g lamb mince
½ small red onion (50g), chopped finely
1 egg yolk
½ cup (35g) stale breadcrumbs
2 tablespoons sumac
1 large loaf turkish bread (430g)
250g tzatziki
350g watercress, trimmed
¼ cup (60ml) lemon juice
225g can sliced beetroot, drained

1 Combine lamb, onion, egg yolk, breadcrumbs and half the sumac in medium bowl; shape mixture into four patties.
2 Cook patties on heated oiled barbecue (or grill plate) until cooked through.
3 Meanwhile, trim and discard ends from bread; cut remaining bread into quarters then halve pieces horizontally. Toast, cut-sides down, on barbecue.
4 Combine remaining sumac and tzatziki in small bowl. Combine watercress and juice in another bowl.
5 Sandwich patties, tzatziki mixture, beetroot and watercress between toast.

note **Tzatziki is a Greek dip made with yogurt, cucumber, garlic and sometimes chopped fresh mint. You can buy tzatziki ready-made in supermarkets and delis.**

TANDOORI LAMB WITH FRESH MELON AND COCONUT CHUTNEY

prep & cook time **25 minutes** serves **4**
nutritional count per serving **27.3g total fat**
(13.5g saturated fat); 1601kJ (383 cal);
13.2g carbohydrate; 18.9g protein; 5.7g fibre

¼ cup (75g) tandoori paste
¼ cup (70g) yogurt
12 french-trimmed lamb cutlets (600g)
1 cup (110g) coarsely grated fresh coconut
½ large firm honeydew melon (850g), grated coarsely, drained
2 tablespoons finely chopped fresh mint
1 tablespoon lemon juice

1 Combine paste, yogurt and lamb in large bowl; turn to coat lamb in mixture. Cook lamb on heated oiled barbecue (or grill plate) until cooked as desired.
2 Meanwhile, combine coconut, melon, mint and juice in medium bowl. Serve coconut chutney with lamb.
serve with **pappadums and lemon wedges.**

note **If fresh coconut is unavailable, use 1 cup finely shredded dried coconut.**

spiced lamb burger with tzatziki

barbecued lamb cutlets with beetroot walnut salad

BARBECUED LAMB CUTLETS WITH BEETROOT WALNUT SALAD

prep & cook time **20 minutes** serves **4**
nutritional count per serving **38.3g total fat**
(13.9g saturated fat); 2178kJ (521 cal);
17.9g carbohydrate; 24.8g protein; 4.6g fibre

¼ cup (60ml) sweet chilli sauce
2 tablespoons barbecue sauce
2 teaspoons worcestershire sauce
2 tablespoons white wine vinegar
12 french-trimmed lamb cutlets (600g)
200g fresh green beans
425g can whole baby beetroot,
    drained, halved
120g firm blue cheese, crumbled
⅓ cup (35g) walnuts, roasted
lemon vinaigrette
1½ tablespoons lemon juice
2 tablespoons olive oil
1 teaspoon caster sugar

1 Make lemon vinaigrette.
2 Combine sauces, vinegar and lamb in large bowl. Stand 5 minutes.
3 Meanwhile, boil, steam or microwave beans until tender; drain. Combine beans in medium bowl with vinaigrette, beetroot, cheese and nuts.
4 Cook lamb on heated oiled barbecue (or grill plate) until cooked as desired. Serve lamb with salad.
lemon vinaigrette Whisk ingredients in small jug.

LAMB STACK WITH CAPSICUM, EGGPLANT AND PESTO

prep & cook time **45 minutes** serves **4**
nutritional count per serving **55.1g total fat**
(13.5g saturated fat); 2959kJ (708 cal);
5.7g carbohydrate; 47.3g protein; 3.5g fibre

2 medium red capsicums (400g)
1 small eggplant (230g), cut into
    8 slices crossways
4 lamb backstraps (800g)
pesto
¼ cup (20g) finely grated parmesan cheese
¼ cup (40g) roasted pine nuts
1 clove garlic, quartered

lamb stack with capsicum, eggplant and pesto

½ cup (125ml) olive oil
1 cup firmly packed fresh basil leaves
1 tablespoon lemon juice

1 Make pesto.
2 Quarter capsicums; discard seeds and membranes. Roast under hot grill, skin-side up, until skin blisters and blackens. Cover capsicum pieces with plastic or paper for 5 minutes, then peel away skin.
3 Cook eggplant on heated oiled barbecue (or grill plate) until tender.
4 Cook lamb, in batches, on heated oiled barbecue until cooked. Cover, stand 5 minutes then slice lamb thickly.
5 Assemble eggplant, lamb and capsicum stacks on serving plates; spoon pesto over each stack.
pesto Blend or process cheese, nuts and garlic and half the oil until combined. Add basil and remaining oil; blend until pesto forms a smooth, thick puree. Stir in juice.

lemon grass lamb with vietnamese vermicelli salad

LEMON GRASS LAMB WITH VIETNAMESE VERMICELLI SALAD

prep & cook time **45 minutes** serves **4**
nutritional count per serving **22.9g total fat**
(7.2g saturated fat); 1856kJ (444 cal);
20.6g carbohydrate; 35.9g protein; 6g fibre

10cm stick fresh lemon grass (20g),
    chopped finely
2 tablespoons light soy sauce
1 tablespoon brown sugar
2 tablespoons vegetable oil
3 lamb backstraps (600g)
70g rice vermicelli
2 lebanese cucumbers (260g), seeded,
    sliced thinly
½ small pineapple (450g), chopped coarsely
1 cup (80g) bean sprouts
1 cup loosely packed fresh coriander leaves
1 cup loosely packed fresh mint leaves
1 large carrot (180g), grated coarsely
1 large butter lettuce, trimmed,
    leaves separated
chilli lime dressing
¼ cup (60ml) hot water
2 tablespoons fish sauce
1 tablespoon brown sugar
2 tablespoons lime juice
2 fresh small red thai chillies, chopped finely
1 clove garlic, crushed

1 Make chilli lime dressing.
2 Combine lemon grass, sauce, sugar, oil and lamb in medium bowl; turn to coat in mixture.
3 Place vermicelli in medium heatproof bowl; cover with boiling water. Stand until just tender; drain. Rinse under cold water; drain.
4 Combine vermicelli, cucumber, pineapple, sprouts, herbs, carrot and 2 tablespoons of the dressing in large bowl; toss gently.
5 Cook lamb on heated oiled barbecue until cooked. Cover; stand 5 minutes then slice thinly.
6 Top lettuce with salad then lamb; drizzle with remaining dressing.
chilli lime dressing Combine ingredients in screw-top jar; shake well.

LAMB WITH CAPSICUM MAYO

prep & cook time **35 minutes** serves **4**
nutritional count per serving **49.7g total fat**
(19.5g saturated fat); 3420kJ (817 cal);
43.3g carbohydrate; 47.5g protein; 4.2g fibre

100g roasted capsicum
½ cup (150g) mayonnaise
8 lamb mid-loin chops (800g)
fetta and olive mash
1kg potatoes, chopped coarsely
⅔ cup (160ml) buttermilk, warmed
1 cup (200g) crumbled fetta cheese
½ cup (60g) thinly sliced seeded black olives
1 tablespoon olive oil

1 Make fetta and olive mash.
2 Meanwhile, blend or process capsicum and mayonnaise until smooth.
3 Cook lamb, in batches, on heated oiled barbecue (or grill plate) until cooked as desired.
4 Top lamb with capsicum mayonnaise; serve with fetta and olive mash.
fetta and olive mash Boil, steam or microwave potato until tender; drain. Mash potato with buttermilk in large bowl until smooth. Stir in cheese and olives; drizzle with oil.

lamb with capsicum mayo

balsamic lamb with fattoush

BALSAMIC LAMB WITH FATTOUSH

prep & cook time **35 minutes** serves **4**
nutritional count per serving **27.9g total fat**
(8.4g saturated fat); 2098kJ (502 cal);
24.6g carbohydrate; 37.3g protein; 3.5g fibre

8 lamb loin chops (800g)
¼ cup (60ml) balsamic vinegar
1 tablespoon olive oil
2 cloves garlic, crushed
fattoush
2 large pitta breads
1 lebanese cucumber (130g), seeded,
sliced thinly
3 medium tomatoes (450g), seeded,
sliced thinly
1 small red onion (100g), sliced thinly
2 green onions, sliced thickly
2 tablespoons olive oil
¼ cup (60ml) lemon juice
1 clove garlic, crushed
½ teaspoon sweet paprika

1 Preheat oven to 220°C/200°C fan-forced.
2 Brush lamb with combined vinegar, oil and
garlic. Cook lamb on heated oiled barbecue
(or grill plate) until cooked as desired. Cover
to keep warm.
3 Meanwhile, make fattoush. Serve lamb
with fattoush.
fattoush Toast bread in oven about 5 minutes
or until crisp. Place remaining ingredients in
large bowl. Break bread into pieces over salad;
toss gently to combine.

GRILLED LAMB WITH BROAD BEAN AND BEETROOT SALAD

prep & cook time **30 minutes** serves **4**
nutritional count per serving **17.4g total fat**
(5.3g saturated fat); 1739kJ (416 cal);
9.3g carbohydrate; 52g protein; 7g fibre

2 cups (300g) frozen broad beans
450g can baby beetroots, drained, quartered
60g rocket leaves
4 lamb backstraps (800g)
anchovy dressing
6 drained anchovy fillets, chopped finely

grilled lamb with broad bean and beetroot salad

1 tablespoon rinsed, drained baby capers,
chopped finely
2 tablespoons olive oil
2 teaspoons finely grated lemon rind
1 teaspoon dijon mustard
1 tablespoon red wine vinegar

1 Boil, steam or microwave broad beans until
tender; drain. Peel away grey-coloured outer
shells; place beans in large bowl with beetroot
and rocket.
2 Meanwhile, make anchovy dressing. Add
2 tablespoons of the dressing to bowl with
salad; toss gently to combine.
3 Cook lamb on heated oiled barbecue (or grill
plate), brushing occasionally with remaining
dressing, until cooked as desired. Serve lamb
with salad.
anchovy dressing Combine ingredients in
small bowl.

CHAR SUI AND HONEY LAMB

prep & cook time **15 minutes** serves **4**

Combine 2 tablespoons char sui sauce,
2 teaspoons peanut oil, 1 tablespoon honey
and 2 tablespoons grated fresh ginger in
large bowl; add 8 lamb cutlets, turn to coat
in mixture, stand 10 minutes. Drain cutlets;
cook on heated oiled barbecue (or grill plate)
until cooked as desired.

BALSAMIC MUSTARD LAMB

prep & cook time **10 minutes** serves **4**

Combine 1 crushed garlic clove, 1 tablespoon
wholegrain mustard, 1 tablespoon balsamic
vinegar and 2 teaspoons olive oil in large bowl;
add 8 lamb cutlets, turn to coat in mixture,
stand 10 minutes. Drain cutlets; cook on
heated oiled barbecue (or grill plate) until
cooked as desired.

FAST CUTLETS

CHILLI LEMON GRASS LAMB

prep & cook time **15 minutes** serves **4**

Combine 1 crushed garlic clove, 2 teaspoons finely chopped lemon grass, 1 finely chopped fresh small red thai chilli, 1 tablespoon fish sauce and 2 teaspoons peanut oil in large bowl; add 8 lamb cutlets, turn to coat in mixture, stand 10 minutes. Drain cutlets; cook on heated oiled barbecue (or grill plate) until cooked as desired.

TANDOORI LAMB CUTLETS

prep & cook time **15 minutes** serves **4**

Mix ½ cup tandoori paste with ¼ cup yogurt; add 8 lamb cutlets, turn to coat in mixture, stand 10 minutes. Cook cutlets on heated oiled barbecue (or grill plate) until cooked as desired. Serve cutlets with 2 tablespoons extra yogurt and sprinkle with ½ finely chopped cucumber.

PORK SCHNITZEL WITH PESTO BUTTER

prep & cook time 35 minutes   serves 4
nutritional count per serving 44.2g total fat
(15.3g saturated fat); 2842kJ (680 cal);
17.8g carbohydrate; 51.9g protein; 3.6g fibre

⅓ cup (80ml) lemon juice
2 tablespoons olive oil
3 cloves garlic, crushed
1 tablespoon fresh thyme leaves
8 pork schnitzels (800g)
500g kipfler potatoes, unpeeled, halved
pesto butter
60g butter, softened
⅓ cup coarsely chopped fresh basil
¼ cup (40g) roasted pine nuts
1 clove garlic, quartered
2 tablespoons coarsely grated
    parmesan cheese

1 Combine juice, oil, garlic, thyme and pork in
medium bowl; toss pork to coat in mixture.
2 Meanwhile, boil, steam or microwave potato
until tender; drain.
3 Make pesto butter. Toss half the pesto butter
with potato in medium bowl; cover to keep warm.
4 Cook pork on heated oiled barbecue (or grill
plate) until cooked as desired. Drizzle pork with
remaining pesto butter; serve with potato.
pesto butter Blend or process ingredients
until smooth.

PORK

pork and corn salsa tortilla wraps

CHINESE BARBECUED PORK

prep & cook time **30 minutes (+ refrigeration)** serves **6**
nutritional count per serving **13.5g total fat**
(4.5g saturated fat); 1321kJ (316 cal);
11.3g carbohydrate; 35.9g protein; 0.4g fibre

1kg pork scotch fillet
2 star anise, crushed
2 tablespoons light soy sauce
2 tablespoons brown sugar
1½ tablespoons honey
1½ tablespoons dry sherry
2 teaspoons hoisin sauce
2cm piece fresh ginger (10g), grated
1 clove garlic, crushed
2 green onions, chopped finely
few drops red food colouring

1 Cut pork into quarters.
2 Combine remaining ingredients in large shallow dish; add pork, turn to coat in marinade. Cover; refrigerate 3 hours or overnight.
3 Drain pork; reserve marinade. Cook pork on heated oiled barbecue (or grill plate) until browned and cooked through, brushing with reserved marinade during cooking.

PORK AND CORN SALSA TORTILLA WRAPS

prep & cook time **30 minutes** serves **4**
nutritional count per serving **24.6g total fat**
(8.8g saturated fat); 2395kJ (573 cal);
46.1g carbohydrate; 41.5g protein; 8.4g fibre

2 tablespoons vegetable oil
35g packet taco seasoning mix
600g pork fillet, sliced thinly
16 x 15cm corn tortillas (400g)
310g can corn kernels, drained
3 medium tomatoes (450g), chopped coarsely
1 small red onion (100g), chopped finely
½ cup coarsely chopped fresh coriander
1 butter lettuce, torn
½ cup (120g) light sour cream

1 Combine oil, seasoning and pork in medium bowl; toss to coat in mixture. Cook pork on heated oiled barbecue until cooked as desired.
2 Wrap tortillas in foil; heat on barbecue (or grill plate) until warmed through.
3 To make corn salsa, combine corn, tomato, onion and coriander in medium bowl.
4 Divide pork, salsa and remaining ingredients among tortillas; roll to enclose filling.

chinese barbecued pork

mexican pork cutlets with avocado salsa

MEXICAN PORK CUTLETS WITH AVOCADO SALSA

prep & cook time **20 minutes** serves **4**
nutritional count per serving **42.2g total fat
(10.7g saturated fat); 2241kJ (536 cal);
1.2g carbohydrate; 38g protein; 1.2g fibre**

**2 tablespoons taco seasoning mix
¼ cup (60ml) olive oil
4 x 235g pork cutlets
3 small tomatoes (270g), seeded,
    chopped finely
1 small avocado (200g), chopped finely
1 lebanese cucumber (130g), seeded,
    chopped finely
1 tablespoon lime juice**

1 Combine seasoning, 2 tablespoons of the oil
and pork in large bowl. Cook pork on heated
oiled barbecue (or grill plate) until cooked.
2 Meanwhile, combine remaining oil in medium
bowl with tomato, avocado, cucumber and
juice. Serve pork with salsa.

grilled loin chops with apple and onion plum sauce

GRILLED LOIN CHOPS WITH APPLE AND ONION PLUM SAUCE

prep & cook time **30 minutes** serves **4**
nutritional count per serving **29.7g total fat
(9.1g saturated fat); 2404kJ (575 cal);
32g carbohydrate; 45g protein; 1.8g fibre**

**2 medium apples (300g)
1 tablespoon olive oil
1 medium red onion (170g), cut into thin
    wedges
4 x 280g pork loin chops
½ cup (125ml) plum sauce
¼ cup (60ml) lemon juice
⅓ cup (80ml) chicken stock**

1 Cut each unpeeled, uncored apple horizontally
into four slices. Heat oil in grill pan; cook apple
and onion, turning, until softened.
2 Meanwhile, cook pork on heated oiled
barbecue (or grill plate) until cooked.
3 Stir sauce, juice and stock into apple mixture;
simmer 1 minute. Serve pork with sauce.

glazed pork cutlets with celeriac salad

GLAZED PORK CUTLETS WITH CELERIAC SALAD

prep & cook time **20 minutes** serves **4**
nutritional count per serving **37.8g total fat**
(9.6g saturated fat); 2441kJ (584 cal);
15.5g carbohydrate; 45.6g protein; 9g fibre

2 teaspoons honey
1 teaspoon dijon mustard
1 tablespoon olive oil
4 pork cutlets (1kg)
400g baby carrots, trimmed
650g celeriac, grated coarsely
⅓ cup (100g) mayonnaise
1 clove garlic, crushed
⅓ cup (80g) light sour cream
2 tablespoons lemon juice
½ cup coarsely chopped fresh
　flat-leaf parsley
2 teaspoons dijon mustard, extra

1 Whisk honey, mustard and oil in large bowl, add pork; toss pork to coat in mixture. Cook pork on heated oiled barbecue (or grill plate) until cooked as desired. Cover pork; stand 5 minutes.
2 Meanwhile, boil, steam or microwave carrots

until just tender; drain. Cover to keep warm.
3 Combine celeriac, mayonnaise, garlic, sour cream, juice, parsley and extra mustard in medium bowl.
4 Serve cutlets with carrots and salad.

BARBECUED PORK NECK WITH FIVE-SPICE STAR-ANISE GLAZE

prep & cook time **1 hour 35 minutes**
(+ standing) serves **6**
nutritional count per serving **13.4g total fat**
(4.5g saturated fat); 1714kJ (410 cal);
36.4g carbohydrate; 36.5g protein; 0.6g fibre

1kg piece pork neck
1 clove garlic, sliced thinly
4cm piece fresh ginger (20g), sliced thinly
2 x 100g packets baby asian greens
five-spice star-anise glaze
1¼ cups (310ml) water
1 cup (220g) firmly packed brown sugar
3 fresh long red chillies, chopped finely
1 star anise
1 teaspoon five-spice powder
⅓ cup (80ml) light soy sauce
¼ cup (60ml) rice vinegar

1 Make five-spice star-anise glaze. Reserve 1 cup of glaze.
2 Make several shallow cuts in pork. Press garlic and ginger into cuts; brush ¼ cup of the remaining glaze over pork.
3 Cook pork on heated oiled barbecue (or grill plate), covered, over low heat, 30 minutes. Turn pork; cook, covered, 30 minutes. Increase heat to high; cook, uncovered, 5 minutes, turning and brushing constantly with remaining glaze. Remove pork from heat. Cover; stand 15 minutes then slice thickly.
4 Meanwhile, place reserved glaze in small saucepan; simmer about 5 minutes or until thickened slightly. Cool.
5 Combine baby asian greens with glaze in medium bowl; serve with pork.
five-spice star-anise glaze Combine the water and sugar in medium saucepan; simmer about 10 minutes or until glaze thickens slightly. Remove from heat; stir in remaining ingredients.

barbecued pork neck with five-spice star-anise glaze

teriyaki pork with pineapple

TERIYAKI PORK WITH PINEAPPLE

prep & cook time **40 minutes (+ refrigeration)** serves **4**
nutritional count per serving **12.2g total fat**
(4.1g saturated fat); 1371kJ (328 cal);
13.3g carbohydrate; 34.1g protein; 3g fibre

⅓ cup (80ml) mirin
¼ cup (60ml) japanese soy sauce
2 tablespoons cooking sake
2 teaspoons white sugar
5cm piece fresh ginger (25g), grated
2 cloves garlic, crushed
600g pork fillets
1 small pineapple (900g), sliced thinly
2 green onions, sliced thinly

1 Combine mirin, sauce, sake, sugar, ginger and garlic in large bowl; add pork, turn to coat in marinade. Cover; refrigerate 3 hours or overnight.
2 Drain pork; reserve marinade. Cook pork on heated oiled barbecue (or grill plate) until browned and cooked as desired. Cover; stand 10 minutes.
3 Cook pineapple on barbecue about 2 minutes or until soft.
4 Bring reserved marinade to the boil in small saucepan; cook about 5 minutes or until sauce reduces by half.
5 Serve sliced pork with pineapple and onion; drizzle with sauce.

pork sausages with warm pear and witlof salad

PORK SAUSAGES WITH WARM PEAR AND WITLOF SALAD

prep & cook time **30 minutes** serves **4**
nutritional count per serving **88g total fat**
(24.5g saturated fat); 4431kJ (1060 cal);
29.3g carbohydrate; 34.7g protein; 12.1g fibre

2 medium red onions (340g), cut into wedges
1 tablespoon caraway seeds
3 medium pears (690g), cut into wedges
¼ cup (60ml) cider vinegar
2 tablespoons olive oil
8 thick pork sausages (960g)
1 cup (120g) pecans, roasted
2 witlof (250g), trimmed, leaves separated,
    halved lengthways

1 Cook onion on heated oiled barbecue flat plate until softened. Add caraway seeds and pear; cook about 5 minutes or until pear is browned lightly. Place pear mixture in medium bowl with vinegar and oil.
2 Meanwhile, cook sausages on heated oiled barbecue (or grill plate) until cooked through.
3 Place nuts and witlof in bowl with pear mixture; toss gently to combine. Serve salad with sausages.

pork burgers with caramelised pears

PORK BURGERS WITH CARAMELISED PEARS

prep & cook time 30 minutes   serves 4
nutritional count per serving 14.2g total fat
(4.2g saturated fat); 2579kJ (617 cal);
79.1g carbohydrate; 37.7g protein; 8.9g fibre

500g pork mince
2 cloves garlic, crushed
3 green onions, chopped finely
1 fresh small red thai chilli, chopped finely
1 egg
2 tablespoons barbecue sauce
½ cup (35g) stale breadcrumbs
4 small pears (720g), sliced thinly
1 medium red onion (170g), sliced thinly
¼ cup (60ml) balsamic vinegar
1 tablespoon brown sugar
1 long french bread stick (300g)
2 tablespoons dijonnaise
50g mizuna

1 Combine mince, garlic, green onion, chilli,
egg, sauce and breadcrumbs in medium bowl;
shape into four patties. Cook patties on heated
oiled barbecue flat plate until cooked through.
2 Meanwhile, cook pear and red onion on
heated oiled flat plate until onion softens. Sprinkle
combined vinegar and sugar over pear and red
onion; cook, turning, about 10 minutes or until
mixture caramelises.
3 Cut bread into quarters; split quarters in half
horizontally. Spread dijonnaise on cut sides;
sandwich mizuna, patties, caramelised pear
and red onion between bread slices.

notes We used small corella pears, with pale flesh and
a mild flavour, for this recipe.
Dijonnaise is a commercial blend of mayonnaise and
dijon mustard; it is available in most supermarkets.

PLUM SAUCE PORK SPARE RIBS WITH PEAR AND CHILLI SALAD

prep & cook time 45 minutes (+ refrigeration) serves 4
nutritional count per serving 18.1g total fat
(6.6g saturated fat); 2847kJ (681 cal);
56.3g carbohydrate; 69.6g protein; 5.2g fibre

2kg american-style pork ribs
1 cup (250ml) plum sauce
5cm piece fresh ginger (25g), grated
⅓ cup (80ml) oyster sauce
2 star anise
1 teaspoon dried chilli flakes
pear and chilli salad
2 medium pears (460g), sliced thinly
2 fresh long red chillies, sliced thinly
2 green onions, sliced thinly
2 cups coarsely chopped fresh mint
2cm piece fresh ginger (10g), grated
2 tablespoons lime juice

1 Combine pork with remaining ingredients in
large shallow baking dish. Cover; refrigerate
3 hours or overnight, turning pork occasionally.
2 Drain pork; reserve marinade. Cook pork on
heated oiled barbecue (or grill plate) 20 minutes
or until cooked through, turning and brushing
frequently with reserved marinade.
3 Meanwhile, make pear and chilli salad.
4 Boil remaining marinade in small saucepan
about 5 minutes or until thickened slightly.
5 Slice ribs into portions; serve with salad and
hot marinade.
pear and chilli salad Place ingredients in
medium bowl; toss gently to combine.

Soak bamboo skewers in cold water for at least 30 minutes before using to stop them burning during cooking.

LAMB AND ROSEMARY KEBABS

prep & cook time **40 minutes** serves **8**

Pull enough leaves from the bottom of 8 long, thick rosemary stalks to make 2 tablespoons of finely chopped leaves; toss in small bowl with 1 crushed garlic clove, 1 tablespoon lemon juice and 1 tablespoon olive oil. Sharpen trimmed ends of rosemary stalks to a point. Thread 500g diced lamb onto rosemary stalk skewers; brush with rosemary oil mixture. Cook kebabs on heated oiled barbecue (or grill plate) until browned all over and cooked as desired.

LEMON TARRAGON SCALLOP SKEWERS

prep & cook time **15 minutes** makes **8**

Combine 2 tablespoons lemon juice, 1 teaspoon olive oil, 2 teaspoons finely chopped fresh tarragon and 1 teaspoon dijon mustard in a screw-top jar; shake well. Cut a medium lemon into eight wedges. Thread one lemon wedge onto each of eight bamboo skewers. Thread 24 scallops without roe onto skewers. Cook skewers on heated oiled barbecue (or grill plate) about 1 minute each side or until cooked as desired. Serve scallops with lemon tarragon dressing and 80g mesclun.

KEBABS & SKEWERS

PORK FILLET AND PANCETTA KEBABS

prep & cook time **30 minutes** serves **4**

Pull enough leaves from the bottom of 8 long, thick rosemary stalks to make 2 tablespoons of finely chopped leaves; toss in small bowl with ⅓ cup olive oil and 1 crushed garlic clove. Sharpen trimmed ends of rosemary stalks to a point. Cut 600g pork fillet into 16 x 2cm pieces. Halve 8 slices pancetta; wrap one slice around each piece of pork. Cut 1 large red capsicum into 24 pieces. Thread pork alternately with capsicum onto rosemary stalk skewers. Brush kebabs with rosemary oil mixture. Cook on heated oiled barbecue (or grill plate), brushing frequently with rosemary mixture, until browned all over and cooked as desired.

CHICKEN, LEMON AND ARTICHOKE SKEWERS

prep & cook time **35 minutes** serves **4**

Place 2 tablespoons lemon juice, 2 tablespoons olive oil and 2 crushed cloves garlic in screw-top jar; shake well. Cut 2 medium lemons into 24 thin wedges. Cut 500g chicken breast fillets into 3cm pieces. Drain and halve 2 x 400g cans artichoke hearts. Thread chicken, artichoke, 24 button mushrooms and lemon wedges onto 12 bamboo skewers. Cook skewers on heated oiled barbecue (or grill plate) until chicken is cooked through, brushing skewers with lemon oil mixture occasionally.

AMERICAN-STYLE PORK RIBS well-trimmed mid-loin ribs. Also known as spareribs.

BABY ASIAN GREENS packaged mix of baby buk choy, gai lan, choy sum and water spinach. Available from Asian grocery stores and major supermarkets.

BABY BUK CHOY also known as pak kat farang or shanghai bok choy, is much smaller and more tender than buk choy. Has an appealing, mildly acrid taste.

BASIL an aromatic herb; there are many types, but the most commonly used is sweet, or common, basil.

BEAN SPROUTS also known as bean shoots; tender new growths of assorted beans and seeds germinated for consumption as sprouts.

BEEF NEW-YORK CUT STEAKS boneless striploin steak.

BREADCRUMBS stale one- or two-day-old bread made into crumbs by grating, blending or processing.

BROCCOLINI a cross between broccoli and chinese kale; milder and sweeter than broccoli. Each long stem is topped by a loose floret that closely resembles broccoli; from floret to stem, broccolini is completely edible.

BUTTER use salted or unsalted (sweet) butter; 125g is equal to one stick (4 ounces).

BUTTER LETTUCE have small, round, loosely formed heads with soft, buttery-textured leaves ranging from pale green on the outer leaves to pale yellow green on the inner leaves.

CAPSICUM also known as bell pepper or, simply, pepper. Discard membranes and seeds before using.

CARDAMOM available in pod, seed or ground form. Has a distinctive aromatic, sweetly rich flavour.

CHICKEN

drumette small fleshy part of the wing between shoulder and elbow, trimmed to resemble a drumstick.

tenderloin thin strip of meat lying just under the breast.

CHILLI available in many types and sizes. Use rubber gloves when seeding and chopping fresh chillies as they can burn your skin. Removing seeds and membranes lessens the heat level.

green any unripened chilli.

long red available fresh and dried; a generic term used for any moderately hot, long (about 6cm-8cm) thin chilli.

red thai small, medium hot and bright red in colour.

CHINESE COOKING WINE also known as chinese rice wine or hao hsing; made from fermented rice, wheat, sugar and salt. If you can't find it, replace with mirin or sherry.

CORIANDER also known as pak chee, cilantro or chinese parsley; bright-green leafy herb with a pungent flavour. Stems and roots of coriander are also used in cooking; wash well. Also available ground or as seeds; these should not be substituted for fresh coriander as the tastes are very different.

CUMIN a spice also known as zeera or comino.

DAIKON also known as giant white radish. Has a sweet, fresh flavour without the bite of the common red radish.

FISH FILLETS, FIRM WHITE any boneless firm white fish fillet – blue eye, bream, swordfish, ling, whiting or sea perch are all good choices. Check for any small pieces of bone in the fillets and use tweezers to remove them.

FIVE-SPICE POWDER a fragrant mixture of ground cinnamon, cloves, star anise, sichuan pepper and fennel seeds. Also known as chinese five-spice.

FRIED SHALLOTS a staple in the Thai kitchen; they can be purchased already made from Asian grocery stores, or you can make your own by frying peeled, thinly sliced shallots or baby onions until golden brown and crisp.

GAI LAN also known as chinese broccoli gai lam, kanah, gai lum and chinese kale; appreciated more for its stems than its coarse leaves.

GINGER also known as green or root ginger; the thick root of a tropical plant.

pickled pink available from Asian grocery stores; paper-thin shavings of pickled ginger in a mixture of vinegar, sugar and natural colouring.

KAFFIR LIME LEAVES aromatic leaves of a citrus tree; used similarly to bay leaves. A strip of fresh lime peel may be substituted for each lime leaf.

GLOSSARY

LAMB BACKSTRAP the larger fillet from a row of loin chops or cutlets.

LEBANESE CUCUMBER slender and thin-skinned. Probably the most popular variety because of its tender, edible skin, tiny, yielding seeds, and sweet, fresh and flavoursome taste.

LEMON GRASS a tall, clumping, lemon-smelling and tasting, sharp-edged grass; the white lower part of each stem is chopped and used in cooking.

MINCE known as ground meat.

MIRIN a sweet rice wine used in Japanese cooking; not to be confused with sake.

MUSHROOMS
  button small, cultivated white mushrooms with a mild flavour.
  enoki clumps of long, spaghetti-like stems with tiny, snowy white caps.
  oyster also known as abalone; grey-white mushroom shaped like a fan. Has a smooth texture and a subtle, oyster-like flavour.
  shiitake when fresh are also known as chinese black, forest or golden oak mushrooms; are large and meaty and have the earthiness and taste of wild mushrooms. When dried, they are known as donko or dried chinese mushrooms; rehydrate before use.
  swiss brown also known as cremini or roman mushrooms, are light brown with a full-bodied flavour. Substitute with button or cup mushrooms.

NORI a type of dried seaweed used in Japanese cooking. Sold in thin sheets, plain or toasted.

OIL
  olive made from ripened olives. Extra virgin and virgin are the best, while extra light or light refers to taste not fat levels.
  peanut pressed from ground peanuts; this is the most commonly used oil in Asian cooking because of its high smoke point (capacity to handle high heat without burning).
  sesame made from roasted, crushed, white sesame seeds; used as a flavouring rather than a cooking medium.

ONIONS
  green also known as scallion or, incorrectly, shallot; an immature onion picked before the bulb has formed, having a long, bright-green edible stalk.
  red also known as spanish, red spanish or bermuda onion; a sweet-flavoured, large, purple-red onion.
  shallots also called french shallots, golden shallots or eschalots; small, brown-skinned, elongated members of the onion family. Grows in tight clusters similar to garlic.

PEKING DUCK PANCAKES small, crêpe-like pancakes sold fresh, usually in containers holding 20, located in the refrigerated section of most Asian grocery stores. Steam for just a few minutes until warm and pliable.

PRAWNS also known as shrimp.

RED CURRY PASTE a blend of red chilli, garlic, shallots, galangal, lemon grass, salt, shrimp paste, kaffir lime peel, coriander, cumin and paprika. It is milder than the hotter thai green curry paste.

RICE VERMICELLI also known as sen mee, mei fun or bee hoon; similar to bean threads, only longer and made with rice flour instead of mung bean starch.

RICE VINEGAR a colourless vinegar made from fermented rice and flavoured with sugar and salt. Milder and less acidic than regular vinegar.

ROCKET also known as arugula, rugula and rucola; a peppery-tasting green leaf used similarly to baby spinach leaves. Baby rocket leaves are both smaller and less peppery.

SAKE Japan's favourite rice wine, is used in cooking, marinating and as part of dipping sauces. If sake is unavailable, dry sherry, vermouth or brandy can be used as substitutes.

  SAMBAL OELEK (also ulek or olek) Indonesian in origin; a salty paste made from ground chillies and vinegar.

SAUCES
  barbecue a spicy, tomato-based sauce used to marinate or baste, or as a condiment.
  fish also called nuoc nam or nam pla; made from pulverised salted fermented fish, most often anchovies. Has a pungent smell and strong taste, so use according to your taste.
  hoisin a sweet, thick Chinese barbecue sauce made from salted fermented soya beans, onion and garlic.
  soy made from fermented soya beans. Several variations are available in most supermarkets and Asian food stores. We use japanese soy in our recipes.

japanese soy an all-purpose low-sodium soy sauce made with more wheat content than its Chinese counterparts; fermented in barrels and aged. Possibly the best table soy and the one to choose if you only want one variety.

kecap manis a dark, thick sweet soy sauce; the soy's sweetness is derived from the addition of either molasses or palm sugar when brewed.

light soy a fairly thin, pale but salty tasting sauce; used in dishes in which the natural colour of the ingredients is to be maintained. Not to be confused with salt-reduced or low-sodium soy sauces.

oyster Asian in origin, this rich, brown sauce is made from oysters and their brine, cooked with salt and soy sauce, and thickened with starches.

plum a thick, sweet and sour dipping sauce made from plums, vinegar, sugar, chillies and spices.

sweet chilli a comparatively mild, Thai-type sauce made from red chillies, sugar, garlic and vinegar.

teriyaki a Japanese sauce, made from soy sauce, mirin, sugar, ginger and other spices.

vegetarian oyster made from blended mushrooms and soy; available from health food stores and some supermarkets.

SICHUAN PEPPERCORNS also known as chinese pepper. Red-brown aromatic seeds resembling black peppercorns; has a peppery-lemon flavour.

SNOW PEAS also called mange tout ('eat all'). Snow pea sprouts are the tender new growths of snow peas.

SOBA a spaghetti-like, pale brown noodle made from various proportions of wheat and buckwheat flours. Both fresh and dried soba can be found in Japanese food shops and some supermarkets.

SPINACH also known as english spinach and, incorrectly, silver beet. Baby spinach leaves are also available.

STAR ANISE a dried star-shaped fruit of a tree native to China. The pods have an astringent aniseed or licorice flavour. Available whole and ground.

SUGAR
  caster also known as superfine or finely granulated table sugar.

  palm also known as nam tan pip, jaggery, jawa or gula melaka; made from the sap of the sugar palm tree. Light brown to black in colour and usually sold in rock-hard cakes. Substitute with brown sugar if unavailable.

  white a coarse, granulated table sugar, also known as crystal sugar.

TAMARIND the most popular souring agent in Southern India. The pods are collected, de-seeded and dried. Before cooking, the acid flesh is soaked in water and the juice is squeezed out. Available dried or as a concentrate or paste from Indian food stores and some major supermarkets.

TACO SEASONING MIX this packaged seasoning is meant to duplicate the mexican sauce made from oregano, cumin, chillies and other spices.

TURMERIC, GROUND the dried root has a peppery, spicy aroma and a bitter, pungent taste. Known for the golden colour it imparts to the dishes of which it's a part.

VIETNAMESE MINT not a mint at all, but a pungent and peppery narrow-leafed member of the buckwheat family; also known as cambodian mint and laksa leaf (daun laksa).

WASABI an Asian horseradish sold as a powder or paste.

WATER CHESTNUTS resembles a chestnut in appearance, hence the English name. Small brown tubers with a nutty-tasting, crisp, white flesh. Their crunchy texture is best experienced fresh, however, canned water chestnuts are more easily obtained and can be kept about a month, once opened, under refrigeration.

WATERCRESS a member of the cress family, a large group of peppery greens. Highly perishable, so use as soon as possible after purchase.

WOMBOK also known as peking or chinese cabbage or petsai. Elongated in shape with pale green, crinkly leaves, this is the most common cabbage in South-East Asian cooking.

ZUCCHINI also known as courgette; small green, yellow or white vegetable belonging to the squash family.

CONVERSION CHART

MEASURES

One Australian metric measuring cup holds approximately 250ml, one Australian metric tablespoon holds 20ml, one Australian metric teaspoon holds 5ml.

The difference between one country's measuring cups and another's is within a 2- or 3-teaspoon variance, and will not affect your cooking results. North America, New Zealand and the United Kingdom use a 15ml tablespoon. All cup and spoon measurements are level. The most accurate way of measuring dry ingredients is to weigh them. When measuring liquids, use a clear glass or plastic jug with metric markings.

We use large eggs with an average weight of 60g.

DRY MEASURES

METRIC	IMPERIAL
15g	½oz
30g	1oz
60g	2oz
90g	3oz
125g	4oz (¼lb)
155g	5oz
185g	6oz
220g	7oz
250g	8oz (½lb)
280g	9oz
315g	10oz
345g	11oz
375g	12oz (¾lb)
410g	13oz
440g	14oz
470g	15oz
500g	16oz (1lb)
750g	24oz (1½lb)
1kg	32oz (2lb)

LIQUID MEASURES

METRIC	IMPERIAL
30ml	1 fluid oz
60ml	2 fluid oz
100ml	3 fluid oz
125ml	4 fluid oz
150ml	5 fluid oz (¼ pint/1 gill)
190ml	6 fluid oz
250ml	8 fluid oz
300ml	10 fluid oz (½ pint)
500ml	16 fluid oz
600ml	20 fluid oz (1 pint)
1000ml (1 litre)	1¾ pints

LENGTH MEASURES

METRIC	IMPERIAL
3mm	⅛in
6mm	¼in
1cm	½in
2cm	¾in
2.5cm	1in
5cm	2in
6cm	2½in
8cm	3in
10cm	4in
13cm	5in
15cm	6in
18cm	7in
20cm	8in
23cm	9in
25cm	10in
28cm	11in
30cm	12in (1ft)

OVEN TEMPERATURES

These oven temperatures are only a guide for conventional ovens. For fan-forced ovens, check the manufacturer's manual.

	°C (CELSIUS)	°F (FAHRENHEIT)	GAS MARK
Very slow	120	250	½
Slow	150	275-300	1-2
Moderately slow	160	325	3
Moderate	180	350-375	4-5
Moderately hot	200	400	6
Hot	220	425-450	7-8
Very hot	240	475	9

INDEX

ACP BOOKS

General manager Christine Whiston
Editor-in-chief Susan Tomnay
Creative director Hieu Chi Nguyen
Art director Hannah Blackmore
Designer Clare O'Loughlin
Senior editor Wendy Bryant
Food director Pamela Clark
Test Kitchen manager Belinda Farlow
Sales & rights director Brian Cearnes
Marketing manager Bridget Cody
Senior business analyst Rebecca Varela
Circulation manager Jama Mclean
Operations manager David Scotto
Production manager Victoria Jefferys

ACP Books are published by ACP Magazines
a division of PBL Media Pty Limited
PBL Media, Chief Executive officer Ian Law
Publishing & sales director, Women's lifestyle Lynette Phillips
Editor-at-large, Women's lifestyle Pat Ingram
Marketing director, Women's lifestyle Matthew Dominello
Commercial manager, Women's lifestyle Seymour Cohen
Research Director, Women's lifestyle Justin Stone

Produced by ACP Books, Sydney.

Published by ACP Books, a division of ACP Magazines Ltd, 54 Park St, Sydney; GPO Box 4088, Sydney, NSW 2001.
phone (02) 9282 8618; fax (02) 9267 9438. acpbooks@acpmagazines.com.au; www.acpbooks.com.au

Printed by Toppan Printing Co., China.

Australia Distributed by Network Services, phone +61 2 9282 8777;
fax +61 2 9264 3278; networkweb@networkservicescompany.com.au
United Kingdom Distributed by Australian Consolidated Press (UK),
phone (01604) 642 200; fax (01604) 642 300; books@acpuk.com
New Zealand Distributed by Netlink Distribution Company, phone (9) 366 9966; ask@ndc.co.nz
South Africa Distributed by PSD Promotions, phone (27 11) 392 6065/6/7;
fax (27 11) 392 6079/80; orders@psdprom.co.za
Canada Distributed by Publishers Group Canada
phone (800) 663 5714; fax (800) 565 3770; service@raincoast.com

Title: Easy barbecues / food director Pamela Clark.
ISBN: 978 1 86396 857 7 (pbk.)
Notes: Includes index.
Subjects: Barbecue cookery.
Other Authors/Contributors: Clark, Pamela.
Dewey Number: 641.578
© ACP Magazines Ltd 2009
ABN 18 053 273 546

Cover Spicy vegetable kebabs, page 4
Photographer Ian Wallace
Stylist Louise Pickford
Food preparation Rebecca Squadrito

Send recipe enquiries to: recipeenquiries@acpmagazines.com.au